MICROWAVE COOKING FOR 1

by
Rena Croft

foulsham
LONDON • NEW YORK • TORONTO • SYDNEY

foulsham
Yeovil Road, Slough, Berkshire, SL1 4JH

ISBN 0-572-01959-9

Copyright © 1994 Strathearn Publishing Ltd.

All rights reserved.

The Copyright Act (1956) prohibits (subject to certain
very limited exceptions) the making of copies of any
copyright work or of a substantial part of such a work,
including the making of copies by photocopying or similar
process. Written permission to make a copy or copies must
therefore normally be obtained from the publisher in
advance. It is advisable also to consult the publisher if
in any doubt as to the legality of any copying which is
to be undertaken.

Phototypeset in Great Britain by Typesetting Solutions, Slough, Berks.
Printed in Great Britain by St Edmundsbury Press Ltd.,
Bury St Edmunds, Suffolk.

CONTENTS 1

Introduction		4
Chapter 1	Hints and Tips on Microwaving for One	5
Chapter 2	Notes on the Recipes	7
Chapter 3	Soups	8
Chapter 4	Starters and Snacks	14
Chapter 5	Eggs and Cheese	21
Chapter 6	Fish and Shellfish	29
Chapter 7	Poultry	37
Chapter 8	Meat	44
Chapter 9	Vegetables and Salads	54
Chapter 10	Pasta and Rice	68
Chapter 11	Sauces	73
Chapter 12	Desserts	82
Chapter 13	Cakes and Biscuits	90
Index		95

INTRODUCTION 1

For people cooking for one, there is always the temptation not to bother with a 'proper meal' but to settle for a quick snack. With a microwave, however, you can rustle up delicious and nutritious meals with very little fuss and bother, so it makes it really worthwhile to cook in small quantities.

The recipes in this book are especially designed for cooking for one person so you do not have the trouble of calculating a quarter of recipes. Ingredients have been selected so they use a range of meats and vegetables in cuts and quantities which are easy to buy on a small scale. The recipes have also been written as simply and clearly as possible.

If you do want to cook for more than one, simply increase the quantities. If you double the quantity, increase the cooking time by about half as much again, and check the food carefully until it is cooked correctly. It is always better to undercook in a microwave then return the food for a few more seconds or minutes.

So be adventurous and use your microwave to create delicious and nutritious dishes every day of the week.

Chapter One

HINTS AND TIPS ON MICROWAVING FOR ONE

1

Try to plan your week's meals in advance so that you can reduce the number of shopping trips you need and have everything to hand when you want it. It is also easier to make sure you are eating a well balanced diet.

Buy a selection of suitable microwave cookware in small sizes so that your food fits neatly into the container.

Invest in some attractive microwave dishes in which you can both cook and serve to save on time and washing up. Small porcelain gratin dishes, for example, are perfect for cooking and serving an individual portion.

If you have a freezer, it can help you to add variety to your menu. Cook dishes in standard quantities then freeze them in individual portions to eat when it suits you.

If you make chicken stock, freeze it in small containers or in ice-cube trays so that you can defrost exactly the quantity you require. When you buy chops, minced (ground) beef or other similar items, freeze them in individual portions so they are ready to use.

You can also use the freezer to keep a small stock of handy items for quick defrosting in the microwave: bread rolls, pitta breads, sticks of cream, meat and a few frozen vegetables. Look out for packs of freeze-dried herbs which you simply sprinkle from the packet in the quantities you require.

Be careful not to overseason small quantities. Taste as you cook and adjust seasoning accordingly.

Use strongly flavoured ingredients, such as onions or garlic, carefully. If you find onion flavours too strong, substitute shallots. If you only enjoy a hint of garlic, use a sprinkling of freeze-dried garlic instead of fresh.

To crisp up leftover snack foods, place them in a bowl lined with kitchen paper and microwave on High for 20-60 seconds until just warm to the touch. Leave to cool.

If you double the quantities, increase the cooking time by one-third to start with then cook in small bursts until the food is ready.

Always underestimate cooking times as small quantities will easily spoil if overcooked.

Chapter Two

NOTES ON THE RECIPES

1. All the recipes quantities are for one person unless otherwise specified.
2. Follow one set of measurements only, do not mix metric, Imperial or American.
3. Eggs are size 2.
4. Wash fresh produce before preparation.
5. Spoon measurements are level.
6. A tablespoon is 15 ml; a teaspoon is 5 ml.
7. Adjust seasoning and strongly flavoured ingredients, such as onions and garlic, to suit your own taste.
8. If you substitute dried for fresh herbs, use only half the amount specified.
9. Times are based on a 600 watt microwave oven. Cooking times in a microwave vary depending on the temperature of the food when cooking starts, the size and shape of container and so on. Always undercook rather than overcook and test the food regularly during cooking.

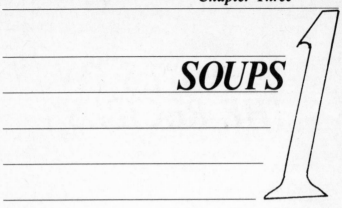

Chapter Three

SOUPS

As an introduction to a meal, or a meal in themselves served with crusty rolls, grated cheese or pitta bread, homemade soups are among the most versatile of dishes for the person cooking for one. Experiment with different ingredients you have available to create an infinite range of tasty meals.

Carrot Soup

Serves 1

Ingredients	Metric	Imperial	American
Butter or margarine	5 ml	1 tbsp	1 tbsp
Shallot, finely chopped	1	1	1
Celery stalk, finely chopped	½	½	½
Lean bacon rasher (slice), rinded and finely chopped	1	1	1
Pinch of sugar			
Salt and freshly ground black pepper			
Carrots, grated or finely chopped	100 g	4 oz	¼ lb
Chicken or vegetable stock	150 ml	¼ pt	⅔ cup
Toasted bread slice, cut into croûtons	1	1	1
Grated orange rind	2.5 ml	½ tsp	½ tsp

1   Place the butter or margarine in a bowl and microwave on High for 30 seconds until melted.

2   Stir in the shallot, celery, bacon and sugar and season with salt and pepper. Microwave on High for 2 minutes.

3   Stir in the carrots and stock and microwave on High for 2-4 minutes until the carrots are tender.

4   Purée the soup in a food processor or blender or rub through a sieve.

5   Reheat in the microwave for about 1 minute. Serve sprinkled with croûtons and grated orange rind.

Courgette and Tomato Soup

Serves 1

Ingredients	Metric	Imperial	American
Courgettes (zucchini), diced	100 g	4 oz	¼ lb
Tomato, skinned and chopped	1	1	1
Milk	120 ml	4 fl oz	½ cup
Pinch of chopped fresh chives			
Salt and freshly ground black pepper			
Single (light) cream	15 ml	1 tbsp	1 tbsp

1 Place the courgettes into a bowl, cover and microwave on High for 1-2 minutes until just tender.

2 Purée the courgettes with the tomato and milk.

3 Return the purée to the bowl, add the chives and season to taste with salt and pepper. Microwave on High for 1 minute then on Medium for 4-6 minutes, stirring once during cooking.

4 Rub the soup through a sieve, then check and adjust the seasoning to taste. Microwave on High for 1-2 minutes to reheat then swirl in the cream before serving.

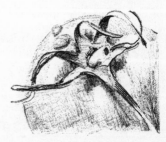

Lentil Soup with Bacon

Serves 1

Ingredients	Metric	Imperial	American
Lentils, soaked overnight	25 g	1 oz	2 tbsp
Chicken stock	250 ml	8 fl oz	1 cup
Bacon rashers (slices), rinded and chopped	2	2	2
Small onion, chopped	½	½	½
Celery stalk, chopped	½	½	½
Salt and freshly ground black pepper			
Chopped fresh parsley	5 ml	1 tsp	1 tsp

1   Drain the lentils and place in a casserole dish with the stock, 1 bacon rasher, the onion and celery. Season with salt and pepper. Cover and microwave on High for 4-6 minutes until soft, stirring twice during cooking.

2   Purée the soup in a food processor or blender, or rub through a sieve.

3   Microwave the remaining bacon on High for 30-45 seconds until crisp.

4   Return the soup to the casserole and microwave on High for 1 minute to reheat. Stir in the parsley and sprinkle with the bacon to serve.

Minestrone Soup

Serves 1

Ingredients	Metric	Imperial	American
Oil	5 ml	1 tsp	1 tsp
Shallot, chopped	1	1	1
Celery stalk, chopped	1	1	1
Carrot, chopped	1	1	1
Minced (ground) beef, crumbled	50 g	2 oz	2 oz
Beef stock	250 ml	8 fl oz	1 cup
Canned chopped tomatoes	100 g	4 oz	¼ lb
Canned cannelloni beans, drained	100 g	4 oz	¼ lb
Pinch of dried oregano			
Bay leaf	1	1	1
Salt and freshly ground black pepper			
Soup pasta	30 ml	2 tbsp	2 tbsp
Grated Parmesan cheese	30 ml	2 tbsp	2 tbsp

1   Mix together the oil, shallot, celery and carrot, cover and microwave on High for 2-3 minutes until tender, stirring once.

2   Stir in the beef and microwave on High for 1-2 minutes until the meat is no longer pink, stirring once.

3   Stir in all the remaining ingredients except the Parmesan, cover and microwave on High for 10-15 minutes until the ingredients are tender and the flavours well blended. Serve sprinkled with Parmesan cheese.

Rich Onion Soup

Serves 1

Ingredients	Metric	Imperial	American
Onions, finely chopped	100 g	4 oz	¼ lb
Butter or margarine	15 ml	1 tbsp	1 tbsp
Plain (all-purpose) flour	5 ml	1 tsp	1 tsp
Beef stock	150 ml	¼ pt	⅔ cup
Salt and freshly ground black pepper			
Milk	60 ml	4 tbsp	4 tbsp
Chopped fresh parsley	5 ml	1 tsp	1 tsp

1 Place the butter or margarine and onions in a casserole dish and microwave on High for 2 minutes until soft, stirring once during cooking.

2 Stir in the flour, then blend in the stock and season with salt and pepper. Microwave on High for 3-5 minutes.

3 Purée the soup in a food processor or blender, or rub it through a sieve.

4 Meanwhile, microwave the milk on High for 45 seconds. Stir it into the onion mixture and microwave on High for about 1 minute. Serve sprinkled with parsley.

Chapter Four

STARTERS AND SNACKS

On many occasions when cooking for one, you will not bother with a proper appetiser to a meal. There are occasions, however, when you will want to make a complete meal, and these recipes are all eminently suitable. There are also times when you will want a light meal or snack, and these delicious dishes are ideal for that, too.

Chick Pea Pâté

Serves 2

Ingredients	Metric	Imperial	American
Olive oil	5 ml	1 tsp	1 tsp
Small onion, chopped	½	½	½
Chopped green pepper	15 ml	1 tbsp	1 tbsp
Pinch of cayenne pepper			
Salt and freshly ground black pepper			
Canned chick peas (garbanzo beans), drained	100 g	4 oz	¼ lb
Water	15 ml	1 tbsp	1 tbsp
Tomato, skinned, seeded and chopped	1	1	1

1   Place the oil, onion, pepper, cayenne and salt and pepper in a bowl and microwave on High for 1-2 minutes until soft.

2   Purée the onion mixture with the chick peas in a food processor or blender, adding just enough water to make a fairly stiff consistency.

3   Return to a bowl and stir in the tomato. Season to taste with salt and pepper. Cover and microwave on High for 1 minute until heated through. Serve with crackers or melba toasts.

Chicken Liver Pâté

Serves 1-2

Ingredients	Metric	Imperial	American
Small onion, chopped	½	½	½
Garlic clove, crushed	½	½	½
Butter or margarine	15 ml	1 tbsp	1 tbsp
Chicken livers	100 g	4 oz	¼ lb
Pinch of ground mace			
Salt and freshly ground black pepper			
Brandy	5 ml	1 tsp	1 tsp

1   Place the onion, garlic and butter or margarine in a bowl and microwave on High for 1 minute, stirring once during cooking.

2   Add the chicken livers and microwave on High for 1-2 minutes until the livers are cooked through, stirring once during cooking. Leave to cool for 3 minutes then season with mace, salt and pepper.

3   Stir in the brandy. Purée the pâté in a food processor or blender or rub through a sieve. Check the seasoning. Press into a serving dish and chill before serving with toast or crackers.

Cheesey Smoked Mackerel

Serves 1-2

Ingredients	Metric	Imperial	American
Butter or margarine	10 ml	2 tsp	2 tsp
Plain (all-purpose) flour	10 ml	2 tsp	2 tsp
Milk	150 ml	¼ pt	⅔ cup
Grated Cheddar cheese	30 ml	2 tbsp	2 tbsp
Pinch of mustard powder			
Salt and freshly ground black pepper			
Smoked mackerel fillet, skinned and flaked	1	1	1

1   Place the butter or margarine in a bowl and microwave on High for 10 seconds until melted. Stir in the flour and milk and microwave on High for about 1 minute, stirring once during cooking. Whisk thoroughly.

2   Stir most of the cheese into the sauce and season with mustard, salt and pepper. Fold in the flaked fish. Place the mixture in a small bowl and sprinkle with the reserved cheese. Microwave on High for 1 minute. Serve hot with toast.

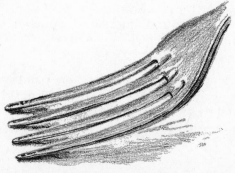

Chinese Meatballs

Serves 1

Ingredients	Metric	Imperial	American
Minced (ground) beef	100 g	4 oz	¼ lb
Garlic clove, crushed	½	½	½
Dried breadcrumbs	30 ml	2 tbsp	2 tbsp
Pinch of mustard powder			
Pinch of ground ginger			
Salt and freshly ground black pepper			
Small egg, beaten	½	½	½
Tomato purée (paste)	45 ml	3 tbsp	3 tbsp
Clear honey	30 ml	2 tbsp	2 tbsp
Soy sauce	15 ml	1 tbsp	1 tbsp
Spring onions (scallions), diagonally sliced	4	4	4

1   Mix together the beef, garlic, breadcrumbs, mustard and ginger and season with salt and pepper. Gradually mix in enough egg to bind the mixture together (you will not need all the egg) then press into small meatballs about 5 cm/2 in in diameter.

2   Arrange the meatballs in a casserole dish, cover with greaseproof paper and microwave on High for 2-4 minutes until firm and no longer pink, rearranging twice during cooking. Drain.

3   Mix together the tomato purée, honey and soy sauce, pour over the meatballs and stir so that the meatballs are covered in the sauce. Cover and microwave on High for 1-2 minutes until hot, stirring once during cooking. Serve garnished with spring onions.

Stuffed Mushrooms

Serves 1

Ingredients	Metric	Imperial	American
Large mushrooms	*2-4*	*2-4*	*2-4*
Minced (ground) beef	*50 g*	*2 oz*	*2 oz*
Pinch of paprika			
Salt and freshly ground black pepper			
Garlic clove, crushed	*½*	*½*	*½*
Dried breadcrumbs	*15 ml*	*1 tbsp*	*1 tbsp*
Chopped fresh parsley	*5 ml*	*1 tsp*	*1 tsp*
Strong cheese slices	*2*	*2*	*2*

1   Use a suitable number of mushrooms, depending on their size. Remove and chop the stems.

2   Season the beef with paprika, salt and pepper and stir in the garlic. Microwave on High for 1 minute until the beef is no longer pink, stirring once during cooking. Drain.

3   Mix the breadcrumbs and parsley into the meat and check and adjust the seasoning to taste. Arrange the mushroom caps on a plate and spoon the mixture into the caps. Cover with greaseproof paper and microwave on High for 2-4 minutes until the mushrooms are soft, rearranging twice during cooking.

4   Top the mushrooms with pieces of cheese and leave to stand for a few minutes until the cheese has melted.

Toasted Beef Snack

Serves 1

Ingredients	Metric	Imperial	American
Mushrooms, sliced	50 g	2 oz	2 oz
Small courgette (zucchini), thinly sliced	1	1	1
Small onion, thinly sliced	1	1	1
Few drops of Worcestershire sauce			
Salt and freshly ground black pepper			
Tomato, skinned and chopped	1	1	1
Minced (ground) beef	50 g	2 oz	2 oz
Pinch of dried basil			
Pinch of dried parsley			
Thick bread slices, toasted	2	2	2
Strong Cheddar cheese slices	2	2	2
Few fresh parsley sprigs			

1   Mix together the mushrooms, courgette and onion and season to taste with Worcestershire sauce, salt and pepper. Cover and microwave on High for 2-3 minutes until the vegetables are tender, stirring once during cooking.

2   Drain the vegetables and stir in the tomato.

3   Mix together the beef and herbs and season with salt and pepper. Microwave on High for 1-2 minutes until the meat is no longer pink, stirring once during cooking. Mix with the vegetables.

4   Divide the beef mixture between the two toast slices and top with the cheese. Microwave on High for 20-30 seconds until the cheese has melted. Serve garnished with parsley.

Chapter Five

EGGS AND CHEESE 1

Many dishes using dairy products are quick and easy to make for one, and can be served as quick snacks, or served with vegetables or salad to create a tasty main meal.

Simple Microwave Eggs

Serves 1

Boiled Egg
Wrap the egg totally in foil and place in a bowl of hot water, making sure that the egg is completely covered with water. Microwave on High for 5 minutes. Remove from the water and leave to stand for 2 minutes before serving.

Hard-boiled (Hard-cooked) Egg

Break the egg into a ramekin dish and pierce the yolk twice and the egg white several times with a cocktail stick (toothpick). Cover with microwave film and microwave on Medium for 1-1½ minutes. Leave to stand and cool before chopping or slicing.

Poached Egg

Pour 150 ml/¼ pt/⅔ cup of water into a ramekin dish with a dash of vinegar and salt. Microwave on High for 1½ minutes. Break an egg into the hot water and pierce the egg yolk twice and the white several times with a cocktail stick (toothpick). Cover with microwave film and microwave on Medium for 30-45 seconds. Leave to stand for 1 minute before serving.

Scrambled Eggs

Whisk 2 eggs with a teaspoonful of milk and season with salt and pepper. Microwave on High for 1-1½ minutes, stirring half way through cooking. Leave to stand for 1-2 minutes before serving.

Fried Eggs

Heat a browning dish on High for 5 minutes. Add 30 ml/ 2 tbsp of oil and microwave on High for 1 minute. Break in the eggs and prick the yolks with a cocktail stick (toothpick). Microwave on High for about 30 seconds. Larger eggs may take a few seconds longer, but do not overcook fried eggs otherwise they will explode.

Piperade

Serves 1

Ingredients	Metric	Imperial	American
Ripe tomatoes, halved	2	2	2
Olive oil	5 ml	1 tsp	1 tsp
Green pepper, chopped	½	½	½
Small onion, sliced	1	1	1
Garlic clove, crushed	½	½	½
Pinch of dried oregano			
Few drops of tabasco sauce			
Salt and freshly ground black pepper			
Eggs, beaten	2	2	2
Few sprigs of fresh parsley			
Bread slices, toasted	2	2	2

1　Place the tomatoes on a plate and microwave on High for 1 minute. Leave to cool slightly, then peel off the skins and chop the flesh.

2　Mix together the tomatoes, oil, pepper, onion and garlic and microwave on Medium for 2-3 minutes until just soft. Season with oregano, tabasco, salt and pepper.

3　Season the eggs lightly with salt and pepper. Pour over the vegetable mixture and microwave on Medium for 1-3 minutes until the egg is cooked but still creamy, stirring regularly during cooking. Garnish with parsley and serve with toast.

Baked Eggs with Salami

Serves 1

Ingredients	Metric	Imperial	American
Butter or margarine	15 ml	1 tbsp	1 tbsp
Garlic clove, crushed	½	½	½
Salami, cut into strips	25 g	1 oz	1 oz
Small red pepper, chopped	½	½	½
Egg	1	1	1
Salt and freshly ground black pepper			
Single (light) cream	15 ml	1 tbsp	1 tbsp

1   Place the butter in a large ramekin dish and microwave on High for 10 seconds until melted.

2   Stir in the garlic, salami and pepper, cover and microwave on High for 1-2 minutes, stirring once during cooking.

3   Break the egg into the bowl and prick the yolk and white with a cocktail stick (toothpick). Season with salt and pepper and spoon over the cream. Cover and microwave on Medium for 1-2 minutes until the egg is set, checking once during cooking.

Tasty Cheese Bread

Serves 1

Ingredients	Metric	Imperial	American
Plain (all-purpose) flour	*50 g*	*2 oz*	*½ cup*
Baking powder	*2.5 ml*	*½ tsp*	*½ tsp*
Pinch of mustard powder			
Pinch of salt			
Cheddar cheese, grated	*50 g*	*2 oz*	*½ cup*
Butter or margarine	*15 ml*	*1 tbsp*	*1 tbsp*
Egg, lightly beaten	*1*	*1*	*1*

1   Mix together the flour, baking powder, mustard and salt. Stir in one-quarter of the cheese and the butter or margarine.

2   Mix the egg into the dry ingredients and turn into an individual loaf dish. Microwave on High for 2-4 minutes until springy.

3   Sprinkle with the remaining cheese, loosely cover with foil and leave to stand for 10 minutes before serving.

Quiche Lorraine

This recipe freezes well so you can store it in single portions if you wish.

Serves 4

Ingredients	Metric	Imperial	American
For the pastry			
Plain (all-purpose) flour	*100 g*	*4 oz*	*1 cup*
Pinch of salt			
Butter or margarine	*25 g*	*1 oz*	*2 tbsp*
Lard	*25 g*	*1 oz*	*2 tbsp*
Cold water	*45 ml*	*3 tbsp*	*3 tbsp*
For the filling			
Bacon rashers (slices), rinded	*4*	*4*	*4*
Strong cheese, grated	*50 g*	*2 oz*	*½ cup*
Onion, sliced	*1*	*1*	*1*
Single (light) cream	*450 ml*	*¾ pt*	*2 cups*
Pinch of grated nutmeg			
Plain (all-purpose) flour	*15 ml*	*1 tbsp*	*1 tbsp*
Salt and freshly ground black pepper			
Eggs, beaten	*4*	*4*	*4*
Chopped fresh parsley	*15 ml*	*1 tbsp*	*1 tbsp*

1   Sift the flour and salt into a bowl then rub in the butter or margarine and lard until the mixture resembles breadcrumbs. Gradually mix in just enough water to make a firm dough. Cover and chill for 30 minutes.

2   Roll out the pastry and use to line a 23 cm/9 in flan dish. Cover with kitchen paper and microwave on High for 3 minutes. Remove the paper and microwave on High for 1½ minutes.

3   Place the bacon on a piece of kitchen paper and microwave on High for 2 minutes until crisp. Chop and sprinkle over the pastry case with the cheese and onion.

4   Mix together the cream, nutmeg, flour, salt and pepper and microwave on Medium for 5 minutes, stirring several times during cooking. Stir in the eggs and pour into the pastry case. Microwave on Medium for 4 minutes.

5   Sprinkle with the parsley and microwave on Medium for a further 1-2 minutes until almost set. Leave to stand for 5 minutes before serving.

Emmenthal Fondue

Serves 1

Ingredients	Metric	Imperial	American
Garlic clove	½	½	½
Dry white wine	45 ml	3 tbsp	3 tbsp
Few drops of lemon juice			
Emmenthal cheese, grated	100 g	4 oz	¼ lb
Cornflour (cornstarch)	5 ml	1 tsp	1 tsp
Kirsch	15 ml	1 tbsp	1 tbsp
Salt and freshly ground black pepper			
French bread slices, cubed	4-6	4-6	4-6

1   Rub the cut side of the garlic clove round the inside of a casserole dish. Stir in the wine and lemon juice and microwave on High for about 1 minute until very hot.

2   Stir in half the cheese. Add the remaining cheese and microwave on High for 30 seconds.

3   Blend the cornflour to a paste with the Kirsch and stir into the mixture. Season to taste with salt and pepper. Microwave on High for 1-2 minutes until smooth, stirring several times during cooking.

4   To serve, arrange the bread cubes on a plate with the hot dipping sauce and serve with a green salad.

Chapter Six

FISH AND SHELLFISH 1

Fish cooks beautifully in the microwave and you can take advantage of the increasing variety in the shops and supermarkets to create a range of interesting and varied dishes. If you run out of ideas or time is short, simply microwave your fish and serve it with a tasty sauce.

Mackerel with Gooseberry Sauce

This recipe can be used with any whole fish.

Serves 1

Ingredients	Metric	Imperial	American
Mackerel, about 175 g/6 oz, cleaned	1	1	1
Salt and freshly ground black pepper			
Butter or margarine	15 ml	1 tbsp	1 tbsp
For the sauce			
Gooseberries	100 g	4 oz	¼ lb
Water	45 ml	3 tbsp	3 tbsp
Cornflour (cornstarch)	10 ml	2 tsp	2 tsp
Caster (superfine) sugar	15 ml	1 tbsp	1 tbsp

1   Lay the fish in an oval dish and season with salt and pepper. Dot with butter and cover with microwave film.

2   Microwave on High for 3-4 minutes then leave to stand for 2-3 minutes while you make the sauce.

3   Place the gooseberries and most of the water in a bowl and microwave on High for 2-3 minutes until the fruit is soft, stirring occasionally during cooking.

4   Purée the fruit in a food processor or blender. Blend the remaining water with the cornflour and sugar and stir it into the gooseberries. Return to the bowl and microwave on High for 1-2 minutes.

Cod with Olives

Serves 1

Ingredients	Metric	Imperial	American
Cod fillets, skinned and cubed	100 g	4 oz	¼ lb
Olive oil	5 ml	1 tsp	1 tsp
Small onion, chopped	½	½	½
Garlic clove, crushed	½	½	½
Tomato, skinned and thickly sliced	1	1	1
Salt and freshly ground black pepper			
Chopped fresh basil	5 ml	1 tsp	1 tsp
Dry white wine	30 ml	2 tbsp	2 tbsp
Black olives, stoned	45 ml	3 tbsp	3 tbsp
Chopped fresh parsley	5 ml	1 tsp	1 tsp

1   Place the cod and oil in a dish then stir in the onion and garlic. Cover and microwave on High for 1-2 minutes, stirring once during cooking.

2   Arrange the tomato attractively on top of the dish and season with salt and pepper. Sprinkle with the basil and spoon over the wine. Cover and microwave on High for 45-60 seconds.

3   Carefully stir in the olives and microwave for 30 seconds. Serve sprinkled with parsley.

Stuffed Trout with Orange Sauce

Serves 1

Ingredients	Metric	Imperial	American
Butter or margarine	10 ml	2 tsp	2 tsp
Spring onion, chopped	1	1	1
Button mushrooms, chopped	3	3	3
Chopped fresh parsley	10 ml	2 tsp	2 tsp
Fresh breadcrumbs	15 ml	1 tbsp	1 tbsp
Salt and freshly ground black pepper			
Small egg, beaten	1	1	1
Trout, cleaned	1	1	1
For the sauce			
Butter or margarine	15 ml	1 tbsp	1 tbsp
Caster (superfine) sugar	5 ml	1 tsp	1 tsp
Orange, thinly sliced	½	½	½
Orange juice	30 ml	2 tbsp	2 tbsp
Few drops of lemon juice			

1 Place the butter or margarine and onion in a bowl and microwave on High for 1 minute. Stir in the mushrooms and microwave on High for 30 seconds.

2 Stir in the parsley and breadcrumbs and season with salt and pepper. Mix in just enough egg to bind the mixture; you will not need all the egg.

3 Stuff the trout with the mixture and arrange on a shallow dish. Cover and microwave on High for 2-3 minutes, checking once or twice during cooking. Leave to stand for 3 minutes.

4   Place the butter or margarine and sugar in a bowl and microwave on High for 20 seconds until melted. Stir well, then add the orange slices and microwave on High for 1 minute. Add the orange and lemon juice and microwave on High for about 2 minutes.

5   Spoon the sauce over the trout and serve.

Orange Cod with Tarragon

Serves 1

Ingredients	Metric	Imperial	American
Cod fillets, cut into chunks	175 g	6 oz	6 oz
Dry white wine	30 ml	2 tbsp	2 tbsp
Chopped fresh tarragon	5 ml	1 tsp	1 tsp
Salt and freshly ground black pepper			
Orange, thinly sliced	½	½	½

1   Place the cod in a casserole and spoon over the wine. Sprinkle with tarragon and season with salt and pepper. Arrange the orange slices over the top.

2   Cover and microwave on High for 2-4 minutes until the fish flakes easily when tested with a fork, rearranging once during cooking.

Rolled Sole

Serves 1-2

Ingredients	Metric	Imperial	American
Sole fillets, halved lengthways	225 g	8 oz	8 oz
Pinch of grated lemon rind			
Pinch of cayenne pepper			
Salt and freshly ground black pepper			
Carrot, cut into strips	1	1	1
Courgette (zucchini), cut into strips	1	1	1
Water	15 ml	1 tbsp	1 tbsp
Butter or margarine	25 g	1 oz	2 tbsp
Lemon slices to garnish			

1 Sprinkle the sole with lemon rind, cayenne, salt and pepper and roll up. Arrange in a casserole dish.

2 Place the carrot, courgette and water in a dish, cover and microwave on High for 1 minute until beginning to soften. Drain.

3 Spoon the vegetables over the fish and dot with butter or margarine. Cover and microwave on High for 3-5 minutes until the fish flakes easily when tested with a fork. Serve garnished with lemon slices.

Spicy Prawns

Serves 1

Ingredients	Metric	Imperial	American
Oil	15 ml	1 tbsp	1 tbsp
Small onion, chopped	1	1	1
Small green pepper, chopped	½	½	½
Celery stalk, chopped	1	1	1
Garlic clove, crushed	½	½	½
Plain (all-purpose) flour	10 ml	2 tsp	2 tsp
Salt and freshly ground black pepper			
Tomato purée (paste)	15 ml	1 tbsp	1 tbsp
Few drops of lemon juice			
Few drops of Worcestershire sauce			
Few drops of tabasco sauce			
Bay leaf	½	½	½
Water	75 ml	5 tbsp	5 tbsp
Cooked peeled prawns (shrimps)	100 g	4 oz	¼ lb

1 Mix the oil, onion, pepper and celery in a bowl and microwave on High for 2-3 minutes, stirring once during cooking.

2 Stir in the garlic, flour, salt and pepper and microwave on High for 30 seconds. Stir in all the remaining ingredients except the prawns and microwave on High for 1½-2 minutes until the sauce bubbles.

3 Stir in the prawns, cover and microwave on High for 2 minutes. Serve with rice or pasta.

Prawn Curry

Serves 1

Ingredients	Metric	Imperial	American
Butter or margarine	*15 ml*	*1 tbsp*	*1 tbsp*
Small onion, chopped	*½*	*½*	*½*
Eating apple, peeled and chopped	*½*	*½*	*½*
Plain (all-purpose) flour	*10 ml*	*2 tsp*	*2 tsp*
Curry powder	*2.5 ml*	*½ tsp*	*½ tsp*
Pinch of sugar			
Salt and freshly ground black pepper			
Chicken stock	*120 ml*	*4 fl oz*	*½ cup*
Few drops of lemon juice			
Cooked peeled prawns (shrimps)	*100 g*	*4 oz*	*¼ lb*

1   Place the butter or margarine and onion in a bowl and microwave on High for 2 minutes, stirring twice during cooking. Stir in the apple and microwave on High for 40 seconds.

2   Stir in the flour, curry powder, sugar, salt and pepper, cover and microwave on High for 30 seconds. Stir in the stock and lemon juice and microwave on High for 1-2½ minutes until the sauce is thick, stirring several times during cooking.

3   Stir in the prawns and microwave on High for 1 minute until heated through. Serve with rice.

Chapter Seven

POULTRY

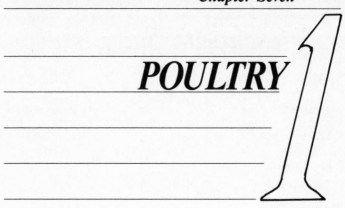

Chicken portions, drumsticks and chicken breast are all ideal cuts of meat for cooking on a small scale: readily available, inexpensive, easy to cook and highly versatile. You can cook them on their own and serve them with a separate sauce, or cook them with sauce ingredients for a moist and succulent dish.

You can also cook chicken portions in a conventional frying pan while preparing a tasty microwave sauce, or team a microwave sauce with ready-cooked chicken.

Small cuts of turkey and duck are becoming increasingly common in supermarkets and are a great way to add variety to your cooking.

Chicken with Spicy Sauce

Serves 1

Ingredients	Metric	Imperial	American
Chicken portion	*1*	*1*	*1*
Butter or margarine, melted	*15 ml*	*1 tbsp*	*1 tbsp*
Salt and freshly ground black pepper			
For the sauce			
Oil	*5 ml*	*1 tsp*	*1 tsp*
Spring onion (scallion), finely chopped	*1*	*1*	*1*
Garlic clove, crushed	*½*	*½*	*½*
Small red pepper, cut into strips	*½*	*½*	*½*
Button mushrooms, sliced	*4*	*4*	*4*
Canned chopped tomatoes	*100 g*	*4 oz*	*¼ lb*
Pinch of dried oregano			
Few drops of chilli sauce			

1   Place the chicken portion in a dish and brush with the melted butter. Season with salt and pepper.

2   Cover with microwave film and microwave on Medium for 8 minutes per 450 g/1 lb. Check during cooking and shield thin portions or bone with small pieces of foil.

3   Mix together the oil, spring onions, garlic and pepper and microwave on High for 2 minutes.

4   Add the remaining sauce ingredients and season with salt and pepper. Microwave on High for 2 minutes, stirring once during cooking.

5   Leave to stand for 5 minutes before serving.

Chicken with Goulash Sauce

Serves 1

Ingredients	Metric	Imperial	American
Boned chicken breast	1	1	1
Paprika			
Salt and freshly ground black pepper			
Shallot, thinly sliced	1	1	1
Plain (all-purpose) flour	2.5 ml	½ tsp	½ tsp
Chicken stock	45 ml	3 tbsp	3 tbsp
Evaporated milk	45 ml	3 tbsp	3 tbsp
Dry white wine	5 ml	1 tsp	1 tsp
Soured cream	10 ml	2 tsp	2 tsp
Chopped fresh parsley	5 ml	1 tsp	1 tsp

1   Cut the chicken breast in half horizontally and arrange in a single layer in a dish. Sprinkle with paprika, salt and pepper and arrange the shallot on top. Cover and microwave on High for 4-5 minutes until the chicken is no longer pink, turning twice during cooking.

2   Blend the flour into the stock, milk and wine and season with a little paprika. Microwave on High for 1-2 minutes until bubbling, stirring several times during cooking.

3   Stir the soured cream into the sauce then pour over the chicken. Sprinkle with a little paprika and serve garnished with parsley.

Chicken with Nutty Rice

Serves 1

Ingredients	Metric	Imperial	American
Boneless chicken breast	1	1	1
Dry white wine	45 ml	3 tbsp	3 tbsp
Long-grain rice	50 g	2 oz	¼ cup
Spring onions (scallions), sliced	3	3	3
Pinch of five-spice powder			
Salt			
Chicken stock	120 ml	4 fl oz	½ cup
Roasted peanuts, chopped	45 ml	3 tbsp	3 tbsp

1   Place the chicken and wine in a bowl, cover and microwave on High for 4-6 minutes until cooked through. Drain, reserving the cooking liquid, and cut the chicken into strips.

2   Place the rice, spring onions, five-spice powder, salt and reserved cooking liquid in a bowl then stir in the stock. Cover and microwave on High for 4 minutes. Stir well then microwave on Medium for about 8-10 minutes until the rice is tender and all the liquid has been absorbed.

3   Stir in the chicken and peanuts and leave to stand for 5 minutes before serving.

Chicken Stir-Fry

Serves 1

Ingredients	Metric	Imperial	American
Boneless chicken breast, cut into strips	1	1	1
Dry sherry	10 ml	2 tsp	2 tsp
Soy sauce	5 ml	1 tsp	1 tsp
Pinch of five-spice powder			
Carrot, cut into strips	1	1	1
Small red pepper, cut into strips	1	1	1
Mini corn cobs	4	4	4
Chinese leaves, shredded	25 g	1 oz	1 oz
Pineapple slice, chopped	1	1	1
Salt and freshly ground black pepper			

1   Place the chicken, sherry, soy sauce and five-spice powder in a bowl and mix well. Cover and leave to marinate for 1 hour.

2   Place the carrot and pepper in a bowl and microwave on High for 1 minute.

3   Add the corn to the chicken mixture and microwave on High for 2 minutes, stirring once during cooking.

4   Add the carrot mixture and remaining ingredients and stir well. Season to taste with salt and pepper Cover and microwave on High for 2 minutes, stirring once or twice during cooking.

Herbed Chicken Livers

Serves 1

Ingredients	Metric	Imperial	American
Chicken livers	100 g	4 oz	¼ lb
Olive oil	15 ml	1 tbsp	1 tbsp
White wine vinegar	10 ml	2 tsp	2 tsp
Pinch of dried basil			
Bay leaf	½	½	½
Salt and freshly ground black pepper			
Butter or margarine	10 ml	2 tsp	2 tsp
Red pepper, cut into strips	½	½	½
Shallot, sliced	1	1	1

1   Rinse the livers and pat them dry. Place in a shallow dish. Mix together the oil, wine vinegar, herbs, salt and pepper and pour over the livers. Cover and chill for 2 hours.

2   Put the butter or margarine in a shallow dish and microwave on High for 20 seconds until melted. Add the pepper and shallot and microwave on High for 2-3 minutes, stirring once during cooking.

3   Lift the livers from the liquid, add them to the pepper and onion and microwave on High for 1-2 minutes, stirring once during cooking.

4   Discard the bay leaf then add the liquid to the livers and microwave on High for 1-2 minutes, stirring once. Serve with rice or mashed potatoes.

Duck with Sharp Mustard Sauce

Serves 1

Ingredients	Metric	Imperial	American
Duck breast	1	1	1
Salt and freshly ground black pepper			
Butter or margarine	15 ml	1 tbsp	1 tbsp
Small onion, chopped	1	1	1
Red wine	45 ml	3 tbsp	3 tbsp
Lemon juice	20 ml	1½ tbsp	1½ tbsp
Grated rind of lemon	½	½	½
French mustard	5 ml	1 tsp	1 tsp
Fresh parsley sprig	1	1	1

1   Pat the duck dry on kitchen paper and prick the skin with a fork. Sprinkle with salt and pepper Microwave on High for 8 minutes. Check and shield any thinner parts with foil and continue to cook in 1-minute bursts until the duck is just tender. Drain off and reserve 30 ml/2 tbsp of the cooking liquid. Wrap the duck in foil and leave to stand.

2   Place the butter or margarine and onion in a bowl and microwave on High for 1-2 minutes until the onion is soft. Add the wine, lemon juice and rind and mustard and stir together until well blended. Reheat on High for about 1 minute.

3   Arrange the duck on a plate and spoon over the sauce. Serve garnished with parsley.

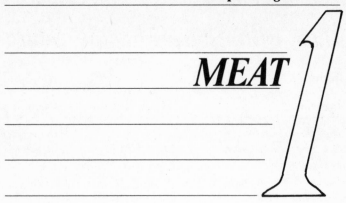

Chapter Eight

MEAT

Minced (ground) beef makes good, quick-cooking dishes for one. You can also use lean braising cuts to make tasty casseroles. Although they have a longer cooking time, you can, if you wish, make slightly larger quantities and freeze them in individual portions. Alternatively, divide fresh meat into individual portions before freezing it for later use.

You can make delicious slow-cooked dishes with lean lamb, use minced (ground) lamb for dishes with rich and tasty sauces, and spice up lamb chops, cutlets and noisettes for all manner of interesting dishes.

Pork chops or slices of spare rib, lean cubed pork or minced (ground) pork all make great basic ingredients for cooking for one in the microwave.

Cheese-Stuffed Beefburgers

Serves 1

Ingredients	Metric	Imperial	American
Minced (ground) beef	100 g	4 oz	¼ lb
Dried breadcrumbs	15 ml	1 tbsp	1 tbsp
Finely chopped onion	5 ml	1 tsp	1 tsp
Few drops of Worcestershire sauce			
Salt and freshly ground black pepper			
Grated strong cheese	30 ml	2 tbsp	2 tbsp
Burger bun	1	1	1
Lettuce leaf	1	1	1
Tomato, sliced	1	1	1

1   Mix together the beef, breadcrumbs, onion, Worcestershire sauce, salt and pepper then divide the mixture in half and press into patties. Place the cheese on top of one half, top with the second and press together into a burger shape, enclosing the cheese.

2   Arrange the burgers on a microwave rack and microwave on High for 2-4 minutes until the meat is firm and no longer pink, turning once during cooking.

3   Cover with greaseproof paper and leave to stand for 1 minute.

4   Slice the bun in half and lightly toast the inside. Assemble the burger with the lettuce and tomato and other relishes or garnish ingredients of your choice.

Chilli con Carne

Serves 1

Ingredients	Metric	Imperial	American
Oil	5 ml	1 tsp	1 tsp
Small onion, chopped	1	1	1
Garlic clove, crushed	½	½	½
Celery stalk, chopped	½	½	½
Carrot, chopped	1	1	1
Minced (ground) beef	100 g	4 oz	¼ lb
Canned red kidney beans, rinsed and drained	100 g	4 oz	¼ lb
Canned chopped tomatoes	100 g	4 oz	¼ lb
Tomato purée (paste)	15 ml	1 tbsp	1 tbsp
Chilli powder	5 ml	1 tsp	1 tsp
Salt and freshly ground black pepper			

1   Mix together the oil, onion, garlic, celery and carrot, cover and microwave on High for 1-2 minutes until just tender, stirring once during cooking.

2   Stir in the beef and microwave on High for 2-4 minutes until the meat is no longer pink, stirring once or twice during cooking.

3   Stir in the remaining ingredients, seasoning to taste with chilli, salt and pepper. Cover and microwave on High for 6-8 minutes until well blended, stirring once or twice during cooking. Check and adjust the seasoning to taste.

Mediterranean Beef Stew

Serves 1

Ingredients	Metric	Imperial	American
Olive oil	15 ml	1 tbsp	1 tbsp
Aubergine (eggplant), cut into chunks	100 g	4 oz	¼ lb
Small courgette (zucchini), sliced	1	1	1
Small onion, sliced	1	1	1
Small red pepper, cut into strips	½	½	½
Chopped fresh basil	2.5 ml	½ tsp	½ tsp
Chopped fresh parsley	5 ml	1 tsp	1 tsp
Pinch of dried oregano			
Salt and freshly ground black pepper			
Minced (ground) beef	50 g	2 oz	2 oz
Canned chopped tomatoes	225 g	8 oz	½ lb

1   Mix together the oil, vegetables and herbs and season with salt and pepper. Cover and microwave on High for 5-6 minutes until the vegetables are just tender, stirring once or twice during cooking.

2   Stir in the beef and tomatoes, cover and microwave on High for 2-3 minutes until the meat is no longer pink and the ingredients are well blended, stirring once during cooking.

Hungarian Goulash

Serves 1

Ingredients	Metric	Imperial	American
Oil	15 ml	1 tbsp	1 tbsp
Small onion, thinly sliced	½	½	½
Lean topside of beef, diced	100 g	4 oz	¼ lb
Tomato purée (paste)	30 ml	2 tbsp	2 tbsp
Canned chopped tomatoes	50 g	2 oz	2 oz
Beef stock	75 ml	5 tbsp	5 tbsp
Plain (all-purpose) flour	10 ml	2 tsp	2 tsp
Paprika	5 ml	1 tsp	1 tsp
Salt and freshly ground black pepper			
Natural yoghurt	15 ml	1 tbsp	1 tbsp

1   Place the oil and onion in a casserole dish and microwave on High for 2 minutes. Stir in the beef and microwave on High for 45 seconds, stirring once during cooking.

2   Stir in the tomato purée and tomatoes. Reserve a spoonful of stock and stir the rest into the dish. Blend the flour with the reserved stock and the paprika then blend it into the dish. Season with salt and pepper. Microwave on High for 6-7 minutes until the sauce is thickened and bubbling and the meat is cooked.

3   Leave to stand, covered, for 3 minutes. Stir in the yoghurt and serve with potatoes.

Lamb Chops with Mango Sauce

This recipe can be used for any lamb chop or cutlet.

Serves 1

Ingredients	Metric	Imperial	American
Lamb chop	1	1	1
Salt and freshly ground black pepper			
Canned mangoes in syrup, drained	100 g	4 oz	¼ lb
Pinch of grated lime rind			
Few drops of lime juice			

1   Place the lamb chop on a plate, cover and microwave on High for 4-6 minutes, turning once during cooking and shielding any thin parts with foil if necessary. Season to taste with salt and pepper.

2   Purée the remaining ingredients in a food processor or blender and serve with the chops.

Kidneys in Wine

Serves 1

Ingredients	Metric	Imperial	American
Butter or margarine	15 ml	1 tbsp	1 tbsp
Shallot, chopped	1	1	1
Button mushrooms, sliced	3	3	3
Lambs' kidneys, halved and cored	3	3	3
Plain (all-purpose) flour	5 ml	1 tsp	1 tsp
Red wine	45 ml	3 tbsp	3 tbsp
Beef stock	15 ml	1 tbsp	1 tbsp
Pinch of French mustard			
Salt and freshly ground black pepper			
Chopped fresh parsley	5 ml	1 tsp	1 tsp

1   Place the butter or margarine and shallot in a bowl and microwave on High for 2 minutes, stirring once during cooking. Add the mushrooms and microwave on High for 30 seconds.

2   Add the kidneys and microwave on High for 1-2 minutes, stirring once during cooking.

3   Stir in the flour then blend in the wine, stock and mustard and season with salt and pepper. Mix well and microwave on High for 2-4 minutes. Leave to stand for 5 minutes. Serve sprinkled with parsley.

Pork Chop with Raspberry Chutney

Use this recipe for any pork chop or cutlet.

Serves 1

Ingredients	Metric	Imperial	American
Pork chop, about 175 g/6 oz	1	1	1
Oil	5 ml	1 tsp	1 tsp
Freshly ground black pepper			
For the chutney			
Raspberries	50 g	2 oz	2 oz
Small onion, chopped	1	1	1
Oil	5 ml	1 tsp	1 tsp
Garlic clove, crushed	½	½	½
Passata (sieved tomatoes)	100 g	4 oz	¼ lb
Tomato purée (paste)	15 ml	1 tbsp	1 tbsp
Soft brown sugar	10 ml	2 tsp	2 tsp
White wine vinegar	10 ml	2 tsp	2 tsp
Salt			

1   Make the chutney in advance. Mix together the raspberries, onion, oil and garlic and microwave on High for 3-4 minutes until tender.

2   Stir in the remaining ingredients, cover and microwave on Medium for 4-5 minutes until thick. Leave to cool, stirring occasionally.

3   Brush the chop with oil and place on a microwave tray. Microwave on High for 3 minutes then on Medium for 6-8 minutes until cooked through. Serve with the chutney.

Spicy Pork Chop

Serves 1

Ingredients	Metric	Imperial	American
Pork chop	*1*	*1*	*1*
Salt and freshly ground black pepper			
Canned chopped tomatoes	*100 g*	*4 oz*	*4 oz*
Carrot, thinly sliced	*1*	*1*	*1*
Shallots, quartered	*2*	*2*	*2*
Raisins	*15 ml*	*1 tbsp*	*1 tbsp*
Tomato purée (paste)	*30 ml*	*2 tbsp*	*2 tbsp*
Pinch of chilli powder			
Pinch of ground cumin			
Pinch of sugar			

1   Place the chop in a dish and season with salt and pepper. Mix together the remaining ingredients and spoon over the chop.

2   Microwave on High for 3 minutes then on Medium for 4-5 minutes until the meat is cooked through, rearranging once or twice during cooking.

Sweet and Sour Pork

Serves 1

Ingredients	Metric	Imperial	American
Canned pineapple chunks	50 g	2 oz	2 oz
White wine vinegar	10 ml	2 tsp	2 tsp
Fresh orange juice	10 ml	2 tsp	2 tsp
Soy sauce	10 ml	2 tsp	2 tsp
Tomato purée (paste)	5 ml	1 tsp	1 tsp
Dry sherry	10 ml	2 tsp	2 tsp
Oil	15 ml	1 tbsp	1 tbsp
Cornflour (cornstarch)	10 ml	2 tsp	2 tsp
Caster (superfine) sugar	10 ml	2 tbsp	2 tbsp
Lean pork, diced	100 g	4 oz	¼ lb
Red or green pepper, sliced	½	½	½

1   Drain the pineapple and reserve 45 ml/3 tbsp of juice.

2   Mix together all the liquid ingredients. Blend in the cornflour and sugar until smooth then stir in the pork and pepper.

3   Cover and microwave on Medium for 7-9 minutes until the meat is cooked through and tender.

4   Stir in the pineapple chunks, cover and microwave on High for 1-2 minutes until heated through.

Chapter Nine

VEGETABLES AND SALADS

You can buy vegetables in any quantity you need – even ones and twos – so it is easy to maintain variety and freshness, even when you are cooking for one.

Jacket potatoes with fillings are a great stand-by. Prick the potato skin and wrap in kitchen paper. Microwave a 175 g/6 oz potato on High for 5-6 minutes.

Everyone's diet should include some healthy salads. They are easy to prepare and can be made to fit with almost any meal, or be served as a meal in themselves. Ready-prepared packs of salad ingredients are obviously more expensive, but for those cooking for one who are short of time, they can save both effort and help to avoid waste. Store salad ingredients loosely wrapped in the bottom of the refrigerator.

Asparagus in Wine

Serves 1

Ingredients	Metric	Imperial	American
Asparagus spears, trimmed	100 g	4 oz	¼ lb
White wine vinegar	10 ml	2 tsp	2 tsp
Olive oil	5 ml	1 tsp	1 tsp
Pinch of chopped fresh parsley			
Pinch of mustard powder			
Pinch of sugar			

1   Arrange the asparagus in a single layer in a dish.

2   Mix together the wine vinegar, oil, parsley, mustard and sugar. Pour over the asparagus, cover and microwave on High for 3-4 minutes until the asparagus is just tender, rearranging once during cooking.

3   Drain and serve, or drain, cover and refrigerate overnight then serve cold.

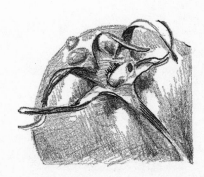

Brussels Sprouts with Lemon Butter

Serves 1

Ingredients	Metric	Imperial	American
Brussels sprouts	100 g	4 oz	4 oz
Water	30 ml	2 tbsp	2 tbsp
Butter or margarine	50 g	2 oz	¼ cup
Grated lemon rind	5 ml	1 tsp	1 tsp
Salt and freshly ground black pepper			

1   Place the sprouts and water in a bowl, cover and microwave on High for 2-3 minutes until just soft but still slightly crunchy.

2   Place the butter or margarine in a bowl and microwave on Medium for 20 seconds until softened. Mix in the lemon rind and season with salt and pepper.

3   Place the butter on the sprouts and toss together until well coated.

Red Cabbage with Apple

Serves 1

Ingredients	Metric	Imperial	American
Bacon rasher (slice), rinded and cut into chunks	1	1	1
Sugar	10 ml	2 tsp	2 tsp
White wine vinegar	10 ml	2 tsp	2 tsp
Pinch of dried oregano			
Salt			
Red cabbage, shredded	100 g	4 oz	¼ lb
Tart eating apple, cored and thinly sliced	1	1	1

1 Arrange the bacon in a dish, cover with kitchen paper and microwave on High for about 2 minutes until crisp.

2 Stir in the sugar, wine vinegar, oregano and salt and microwave on High for 20 seconds.

3 Stir in the red cabbage and apple, cover and microwave on High for 2-3 minutes until the vegetables are just tender, stirring once during cooking.

57

Corn on the Cob with Herb Butter

Serves 1

Ingredients	Metric	Imperial	American
Corn cob	1	1	1
Water	15 ml	1 tbsp	1 tbsp
Butter or margarine	25 g	1 oz	2 tbsp
Chopped fresh chives	5 ml	1 tsp	1 tsp
Chopped fresh parsley	5 ml	1 tsp	1 tsp
Salt and freshly ground black pepper			

1   Place the corn in a bowl and spoon over the water. Microwave on High for 3-5 minutes, turning once or twice during cooking. Leave to stand while you make the herb butter.

2   Place the butter or margarine in a bowl and microwave on High for 20 seconds until softened. Stir in the herbs and season with salt and pepper. Spread over the corn to serve.

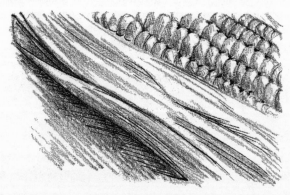

Mustard and Honey Vegetables

Serves 2

Ingredients	Metric	Imperial	American
Butter or margarine	*10 ml*	*2 tsp*	*2 tsp*
Carrot, cut into chunks	*1*	*1*	*1*
Celery stalks, cut			
into chunks	*1*	*1*	*1*
French mustard	*10 ml*	*2 tsp*	*2 tsp*
Honey	*5 ml*	*1 tsp*	*1 tsp*
Few drops of lemon juice			
Freshly ground black pepper			
Button mushrooms, sliced	*2*	*2*	*2*

1 Place the butter or margarine in a small bowl and microwave on High for 10 seconds until melted.

2 Stir in the carrot and celery, cover and microwave on High for 2-4 minutes until the vegetables are just tender.

3 Mix together the mustard, honey and lemon juice and season with pepper. Stir into the vegetables with the mushrooms. Cover and microwave on Medium for 3-4 minutes until tender.

Mushroom and Tomato Potato Filling

Serves 1

Ingredients	Metric	Imperial	American
Shallot, chopped	1	1	1
Mushrooms, sliced	100 g	4 oz	¼ lb
Tomatoes, skinned and chopped	2	2	2
Tomato purée (paste)	5 ml	1 tsp	1 tsp
Chopped fresh basil	2.5 ml	½ tsp	½ tsp
Salt and freshly ground black pepper			
Mozzarella cheese, shredded	50 g	2 oz	2 oz
Jacket potato, baked	1	1	1

1 Mix together all the ingredients except the Mozzarella, cover and microwave on High for 2-3 minutes until the mushrooms are soft and the mixture is well blended.

2 Cut a cross in the top of the potato and arrange on a warm serving plate. Top with the filling and sprinkle with the cheese. Microwave on High for about 1 minute until the cheese melts.

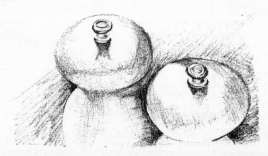

Creamy Prawn Potato Filling

Serves 1

Ingredients	Metric	Imperial	American
Butter or margarine	10 ml	2 tsp	2 tsp
Plain (all-purpose) flour	10 ml	2 tsp	2 tsp
Milk	150 ml	¼ pt	⅔ cup
Tomato purée (paste)	5 ml	1 tsp	1 tsp
Pinch of cayenne pepper			
Salt and freshly ground black pepper			
Cooked peeled prawns (shrimps)	50 g	2 oz	2 oz
Jacket potato, baked	1	1	1

1   Place the butter or margarine in a jug and microwave on High for 10 seconds until melted.

2   Stir in the flour then blend in the milk. Microwave on High for 45 seconds then stir well. Microwave on High for 45 seconds until the sauce is smooth and coats the back of a smooth.

3   Stir in the tomato purée and season with cayenne, salt and pepper. Stir in the prawns and microwave on High for 30 seconds until heated through.

4   Cut a cross in the top of the potato and arrange on a warm serving plate. Top with the filling and serve.

Ham and Vegetable Potato Filling

Serves 1

Ingredients	Metric	Imperial	American
Butter or margarine	10 ml	2 tsp	2 tsp
Shallot, chopped	1	1	1
Plain (all-purpose) flour	10 ml	2 tsp	2 tsp
Pinch of dried dill (dill weed)			
Milk	120 ml	4 fl oz	½ cup
Cooked ham, chopped	50 g	2 oz	2 oz
Frozen mixed vegetables, thawed	75 g	3 oz	3 oz
Salt and freshly ground black pepper			
Jacket potato, baked	1	1	1

1   Place the butter or margarine and shallot in a bowl and microwave on High for 1 minute until soft.

2   Stir in the flour and dill then blend in the milk until smooth. Microwave on High for 2 minutes until the sauce is thick, stirring twice during cooking.

3   Add the ham and vegetables and microwave on High for 1 minute until heated through. Season to taste with salt and pepper.

4   Cut a cross in the top of the potato and arrange on a warm serving plate. Top with the filling, microwave on High for 45 seconds to heat through, if necessary, and serve.

Potatoes Florentine

Serves 1

Ingredients	Metric	Imperial	American
Jacket potato, baked	1	1	1
Frozen chopped spinach, thawed	50 g	2 oz	2 oz
Butter or margarine	10 ml	2 tbsp	2 tbsp
Milk (optional)	15 ml	1 tbsp	1 tbsp
Strong Cheddar cheese, grated	50 g	2 oz	2 oz
Pinch of grated nutmeg			
Salt and freshly ground black pepper			
Egg	1	1	1

1   Slice the top off the cooked potato and scoop out the insides to form a shell.

2   Place the spinach in a sieve and press to remove any excess moisture.

3   Beat the butter or margarine into the potato flesh with just enough milk to make a soft consistency. Mix in the spinach and cheese and season with nutmeg, salt and pepper.

4   Spoon the mixture back into the potato shells and make a hollow in the centre using the back of a spoon. Break the egg into the hollow and pierce the egg whites and yolk twice with a cocktail stick (toothpick). Cover with microwave film and microwave on Medium for 6-8 minutes until the egg whites are firm and the yolks are almost set, checking several times during cooking.

Fruity Scallop Salad

Serves 1

Ingredients	Metric	Imperial	American
Small melon, *cut into chunks*	½	½	½
Olive oil	45 ml	3 tbsp	3 tbsp
Lemon juice	15 ml	1 tbsp	1 tbsp
Chopped fresh parsley	5 ml	1 tsp	1 tsp
Pinch of cayenne pepper			
Freshly ground black pepper			
Bacon rashers (slices), *rinded and chopped*	2	2	2
Scallops	100 g	4 oz	¼ lb
A few lettuce leaves			

1   Mix together the melon, oil, lemon juice, parsley, cayenne and pepper and toss together well. Cover with microwave film and chill.

2   Place the bacon on a plate and cover with kitchen pepper. Microwave on High for 3-5 minutes until crisp and brown. Drain.

3   Place the scallops in a dish, cover and microwave on Medium for 4-5 minutes until opaque, stirring once during cooking.

4   Mix the scallops and bacon into the dressing mixture and serve on a bed of lettuce leaves.

Tuna and Avocado Salad

Serves 1

Ingredients	Metric	Imperial	American
White wine vinegar	30 ml	2 tbsp	2 tbsp
Olive oil	15 ml	1 tbsp	1 tbsp
Pinch of sugar			
Pinch of garlic salt			
Pinch of dried oregano			
Pinch of mustard powder			
Salt and freshly ground black pepper			
Canned tuna, drained	50 g	2 oz	2 oz
Bacon rashers (slices), rinded and cut into chunks	2	2	2
A few lettuce leaves			
Avocado, peeled and sliced	1	1	1
Tomato, cut into wedges	1	1	1

1   Mix together the wine vinegar, oil, sugar, garlic salt, oregano, mustard, salt and pepper. Microwave on High for 1-1½ minutes until boiling.

2   Place the tuna in a small bowl, pour over three-quarters of the hot dressing and stir well. Cover and chill for 2 hours.

3   Place the bacon on a plate and cover with kitchen paper. Microwave on High for 2-4 minutes until crisp. Drain.

4   Arrange the lettuce on a serving plate. Arrange the avocado, tomato, bacon and marinated tuna on top and spoon over the reserved dressing.

Broccoli and Cauliflower Salad

Serves 1

Ingredients	Metric	Imperial	American
Broccoli florets	50 g	2 oz	2 oz
Cauliflower florets	50 g	2 oz	2 oz
Water	45 ml	3 tbsp	3 tbsp
Carrot, grated	1	1	1
Shallot, chopped	1	1	1
Raisins	15 ml	1 tbsp	1 tbsp
Sunflower seeds	10 ml	2 tsp	2 tsp
Natural yoghurt	45 ml	3 tbsp	3 tbsp
Mayonnaise	5 ml	1 tsp	1 tsp
Pinch of grated lemon rind			
Salt and freshly ground black pepper			

1   Place the broccoli, cauliflower and water in a dish, cover and microwave on High for 1-2 minutes until just tender but still crisp. Rinse in cold water then drain.

2   Mix the broccoli and cauliflower with the carrot, shallot, raisins and sunflower seeds.

3   Mix together the yoghurt, mayonnaise and lemon rind and season with salt and pepper. Pour over the vegetables and toss together well to coat. Cover and chill for several hours before serving.

Bean and Vegetable Salad

Serves 1

Ingredients	Metric	Imperial	American
Green beans	50 g	2 oz	2 oz
Celery stalk, sliced	1	1	1
Small red onion, sliced into rings	½	½	½
Water	30 ml	2 tbsp	2 tbsp
Canned red kidney beans, rinsed and drained	100 g	4 oz	¼ lb
Canned cannellini beans, rinsed and drained	100 g	4 oz	¼ lb
Red wine vinegar	15 ml	1 tbsp	1 tbsp
Olive oil	15 ml	1 tbsp	1 tbsp
Pinch of mustard powder			
Few drops of Worcestershire sauce			
Salt and freshly ground black pepper			
Few lettuce leaves			

1 Place the green beans, celery, onion and water in a bowl, cover and microwave on High for 3-4 minutes until just tender, stirring once during cooking. Drain.

2 Mix the canned beans into the beans and celery. Blend together the wine vinegar, oil, mustard, Worcestershire sauce, salt and pepper. Pour over the beans and toss together well. Cover and chill for a few hours before serving on a bed of lettuce.

Chapter Ten

PASTA AND RICE

Pasta, rice and noodles are a convenient store-cupboard staple which are ideal for the single cook as you can prepare them in exactly the quantity you need and use them to create many delicious dishes. You can also buy fresh pasta in many supermarkets. Cook pasta and rice either in the microwave or on the conventional oven. In the microwave, place pasta, rice or noodles in a large bowl and cover with plenty of boiling, salted water. Cover and microwave 100 g/4 oz for 3-4 minutes then leave to stand for a few minutes. If you cook larger quantities, you can use them for cold salads as well as hot dishes.

Pepperoni Pasta

Serves 1

Ingredients	Metric	Imperial	American
Pasta spirals	50 g	2 oz	2 oz
Button mushrooms, sliced	25 g	1 oz	1 oz
Green pepper, cut into strips	¼	¼	¼
Mozzarella cheese, shredded	25 g	1 oz	¼ cup
Pepperoni slices	4-6	4-6	4-6
Minced (ground) beef	50 g	2 oz	2 oz
Pinch of dried oregano			
Salt and freshly ground black pepper			
Canned passata	45 ml	3 tbsp	3 tbsp
Chopped fresh parsley	5 ml	1 tsp	1 tsp

1   Cook the pasta in the microwave (see page 68) or on the conventional oven. Rinse in hot water and drain well.

2   Place the pasta in a large bowl and mix in the mushrooms, pepper, Mozzarella and pepperoni. Keep it warm.

3   Place the beef in a dish and season with oregano, salt and pepper. Microwave on High for about 1 minute until the meat is no longer pink, stirring once during cooking. Drain.

4   Stir the passata into the meat and microwave on High for about 1 minute until hot, stirring once during cooking.

5   Stir the meat into the pasta and serve sprinkled with parsley.

Pepper Noodles

Serves 1

Ingredients	Metric	Imperial	American
Egg noodles	*100 g*	*4 oz*	*¼ lb*
Salt			
Small green, red or yellow pepper, cut into strips (or a combination of colours)	*1*	*1*	*1*
Spring onions (scallions), sliced	*2*	*2*	*2*
Curry powder	*5 ml*	*1 tsp*	*1 tsp*
Cornflour (cornstarch)	*2.5 ml*	*½ tsp*	*½ tsp*
Chicken stock	*75 ml*	*5 tbsp*	*5 tbsp*
Oil	*15 ml*	*1 tbsp*	*1 tbsp*
Cashew nuts	*30 ml*	*2 tbsp*	*2 tbsp*

1   Cook the noodles in boiling salted water either in the microwave (see page 68) or on the conventional oven. Drain.

2   Mix together the pepper and spring onions. Blend together the curry powder, cornflour, stock and oil. Pour over the peppers and mix together thoroughly. Microwave on High for 3-4 minutes until the peppers are just tender, stirring twice during cooking.

3   Stir in the noodles and nuts and serve.

Spinach and Carrot Pasta

Serves 1

Ingredients	Metric	Imperial	American
Pasta shapes	100 g	4 oz	¼ lb
Carrot, sliced	1	1	1
Water	15 ml	1 tbsp	1 tbsp
Fresh spinach, shredded	100 g	4 oz	¼ lb
Oil	5 ml	1 tsp	1 tsp
Soy sauce	2.5 ml	½ tsp	½ tsp
Garlic clove, crushed	½	½	½
Few drops of sesame oil			

1   Cook the pasta shapes in boiling water either in the microwave (see page 68) or on the conventional oven. Drain.

2   Place the carrot and 10 ml/2 tsp of water in a bowl, cover and microwave on High for 2-3 minutes until just tender. Stir in the spinach, cover and microwave on High for about 1 minute until the spinach has wilted. Drain off any excess water. Mix the vegetables with the pasta.

3   Mix together the remaining water, the oil, soy sauce, garlic and sesame oil. Pour over the vegetable mixture and toss together well to coat.

Spanish Rice with Prawns

Serves 1-2

Ingredients	Metric	Imperial	American
Passata (sieved tomatoes)	200 g	7 oz	1 small can
Chicken stock	175 ml	6 fl oz	¾ cup
Long-grain rice	75 g	3 oz	⅓ cup
Spring onion, chopped	1	1	1
Garlic, clove, crushed	½	½	½
Celery stalk, chopped	1	1	1
Tomato purée (paste)	15 ml	1 tbsp	1 tbsp
Pinch of salt			
Pinch of sugar			
Pinch of dried oregano			
Cooked, peeled prawns (shrimps)	50 g	2 oz	2 oz
Chopped fresh parsley	5 ml	1 tsp	1 tsp

1   Mix together all the ingredients except the prawns and parsley in a casserole dish. Cover and microwave on High for 4-5 minutes, stirring once during cooking.

2   Microwave on Medium for 12-15 minutes until the liquid is absorbed, stirring twice during cooking.

3   Stir in the prawns, cover and leave to stand for 3 minutes before serving sprinkled with parsley.

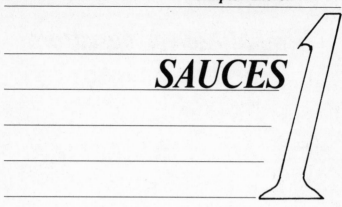

Chapter Eleven

SAUCES

A tasty sauce can turn a simple piece of microwaved fish or grilled meat into a complete and tasty meal. Even if you are in a hurry or have not planned your meal, you can still enjoy something nutritious and tasty.

Simple Sauces based on White Sauce

Makes 150 ml/¼ pint/⅔ cup

Ingredients	Metric	Imperial	American
Butter or margarine	10 ml	2 tsp	2 tsp
Plain (all-purpose) flour	10 ml	2 tsp	2 tsp
Milk	150 ml	¼ pt	⅔ cup
Salt and freshly ground black pepper			

1   Place the butter or margarine in a jug and microwave on High for 10 seconds until melted. Stir in the flour then blend in the milk.

2   Microwave on High for 45 seconds then stir well. Microwave on High for 45 seconds until the sauce is smooth and coats the back of a smooth. Season with salt and pepper.

Variations:

To make **Cheese Sauce:** stir a spoonful of grated cheese and a pinch of cayenne pepper into the finished sauce.

To make **Mushroom Sauce:** add a few sliced mushrooms to the butter and microwave on High for 1 minute then continue with the recipe, adding a few drops of lemon juice with the salt and pepper.

To make **Onion or Shallot Sauce:** add a small sliced onion or a shallot to the butter and microwave on High for 45 seconds then continue with the recipe.

To make **Parsley Sauce:** stir 10 ml/2 tsp of chopped fresh parsley and a few drops of lemon juice into the finished sauce.

To make **Prawn Sauce:** stir 25 g/1 oz of cooked, peeled prawns (shrimps), a few drops of lemon juice and a tea-spoonful of cream into the finished sauce and reheat on High for 30 seconds.

Barbecue Sauce

Serves 1

Ingredients	Metric	Imperial	American
Shallot, chopped	1	1	1
Butter or margarine	10 ml	2 tsp	2 tsp
Plain (all-purpose) flour	5 ml	1 tsp	1 tsp
French mustard	2.5 ml	½ tsp	½ tsp
Few drops of Worcestershire sauce			
Few drops of tabasco sauce			
Dark soft brown sugar	5 ml	1 tsp	1 tsp
Pinch of salt			
Malt vinegar	10 ml	2 tsp	2 tsp
Tomato juice	75 ml	5 tbsp	5 tbsp

1   Place the shallot and butter or margarine in a small bowl and microwave on High for 1-2 minutes. Stir in the flour then blend in all the remaining ingredients.

2   Microwave on High for 3-4 minutes, stirring twice during cooking.

Beef and Mushroom Sauce

Serves 1

Ingredients	Metric	Imperial	American
Button mushrooms, sliced	50 g	2 oz	2 oz
Water	30 ml	2 tbsp	2 tbsp
Cornflour (cornstarch)	2.5 ml	½ tsp	½ tsp
Canned beef consommé	90 ml	6 tbsp	6 tbsp

1   Mix the mushrooms and water in a small bowl and microwave on High for 2-3 minutes until the mushrooms are tender.

2   Blend the cornflour into the consommé then stir it into the mushrooms. Microwave on High for 3-5 minutes until the sauce is thick and clear, stirring several times during cooking.

Cucumber and Dill Sauce

Serves 1

Ingredients	Metric	Imperial	American
Cucumber, cut into chunks	¼	¼	¼
Buttermilk	30 ml	2 tbsp	2 tbsp
Mayonnaise	30 ml	2 tbsp	2 tbsp
Chopped fresh dill	5 ml	1 tsp	1 tsp

1   Place the cucumber in a food processor or blender and purée until smooth. Drain off any excess liquid.

2   Add the remaining ingredients and blend until smooth.

3   Microwave on High for 1 minute until hot.

Onion-Yoghurt Sauce

Serves 1

Ingredients	Metric	Imperial	American
Butter or margarine	*5 ml*	*1 tsp*	*1 tsp*
Spring onion			
(scallions), sliced	*1*	*1*	*1*
Few drops of lemon juice			
Pinch of chopped			
fresh chives			
Pinch of chopped			
fresh parsley			
Mayonnaise	*15 ml*	*1 tbsp*	*1 tbsp*
Plain yoghurt	*90 ml*	*6 tbsp*	*6 tbsp*
Salt and freshly ground			
black pepper			

1   Mix together the butter or margarine, spring onion, lemon juice and herbs in a small bowl and microwave on High for 1-2 minutes until the spring onion is tender but still crisp.

2   Leave to cool slightly, then stir in the mayonnaise and yoghurt and season to taste with salt and pepper.

Tomato Sauce

Serves 1

Ingredients	Metric	Imperial	American
Canned chopped tomatoes	100 g	4 oz	¼ lb
Tomato purée (paste)	15 ml	1 tbsp	1 tbsp
Chopped onion	5 ml	1 tsp	1 tsp
Garlic clove, crushed	½	½	½
Olive oil	5 ml	1 tsp	1 tsp
Pinch of soft brown sugar			
Pinch of oregano			

1   Mix together all the ingredients and microwave on High for 3-4 minutes, stirring occasionally.

Spiced Peach Butter

This sauce will keep in the refrigerator for about 2 weeks in an airtight jar.

Serves 4

Ingredients	Metric	Imperial	American
Small peach, peeled and cut into chunks	1	1	1
Butter or margarine	100 g	4 oz	½ cup
Pinch of cayenne pepper			
Pinch of ground cinnamon			

1 Finely chop the peach either with a knife or in a food processor.

2 Microwave the butter or margarine on Medium for 15-30 seconds until melted.

3 Add the melted butter to the peach in the processor with the cayenne and cinnamon. Process until smooth.

4 Brush on chicken, turkey, beef or pork just before they finish cooking.

Sweet Mustard Sauce

This sauce will keep in the refrigerator for about 2 weeks in an airtight jar.

Serves 4

Ingredients	Metric	Imperial	American
Onion, chopped	1	1	1
Oil	15 ml	1 tbsp	1 tbsp
Mustard seed	10 ml	2 tsp	2 tsp
Clear honey	75 ml	5 tbsp	5 tbsp
Made mustard	60 ml	4 tbsp	4 tbsp
Lemon juice	30 ml	2 tbsp	2 tbsp

1 Mix the onion, oil and mustard seed in a bowl, cover and microwave on High for 2-3 minutes until the onion is soft, stirring once during cooking.

2 Whisk in the remaining ingredients and microwave on High for about 2 minutes until boiling, stirring once or twice during cooking.

3 Brush on chicken, turkey, beef or pork just before they finish cooking.

Butterscotch Sauce

Serves 1

Ingredients	Metric	Imperial	American
Light brown sugar	50 g	2 oz	¼ cup
Butter or margarine	15 ml	1 tbsp	1 tbsp
Evaporated milk	20 ml	1½ tbsp	1½ tbsp

1   Place the sugar and butter or margarine in a bowl and microwave on High for 20-30 seconds until blended.

2   Stir in the evaporated milk and microwave on High for 45 seconds, stirring once during cooking. Pour over desserts or ice cream to serve.

Custard Sauce

Serves 2-3

Ingredients	Metric	Imperial	American
Egg	1	1	1
Plain (all-purpose) flour	40 g	1½ oz	5 tbsp
Soft brown sugar	25 g	1 oz	2 tbsp
Few drops of vanilla essence (extract)			
Milk	600 ml	1 pt	2½ cups

1   Beat the egg, flour, sugar and vanilla essence together.

2   Pour the milk into a separate bowl and microwave on High for 3-4 minutes until steaming.

3   Pour the hot milk on to the egg mixture, whisking all the time.

4   Strain into a clean bowl and microwave on Low for 5-6 minutes until thick, whisking several times during cooking.

Raspberry Sauce

Serves 1

Ingredients	Metric	Imperial	American
Raspberries	*100 g*	*4 oz*	*¼ lb*
Caster (superfine) sugar	*15 ml*	*1 tbsp*	*1 tbsp*
Cornflour (cornstarch)	*5 ml*	*1 tsp*	*1 tsp*
Water	*5 ml*	*1 tsp*	*1 tsp*
Few drops of lemon juice			

1   Rub the raspberries through a sieve to remove the pips.

2   Mix together the raspberries and sugar, adding sugar to taste.

3   Blend together the cornflour and water then stir the mixture into the raspberries. Microwave on High for about 1 minute, stirring once or twice during cooking.

4   Stir in a little lemon juice to taste then leave to cool.

Chapter Twelve

DESSERTS

Fresh fruit, yoghurt or other ready-made products all make excellent, simple desserts when you are cooking for one, but with a little imagination there are plenty of other small-scale desserts you can create quickly and easily in the microwave.

Sponge Pudding with Syrup Sauce

Serves 1

Ingredients	Metric	Imperial	American
Butter or margarine	25 g	1 oz	2 tbsp
Caster (superfine) sugar	25 g	1 oz	2 tbsp
Egg, beaten	1	1	1
Self-raising flour	40 g	1½ oz	6 tbsp
Baking powder	2.5 ml	½ tsp	½ tsp
Golden (light corn) syrup	30 ml	2 tbsp	2 tbsp

1   Mix together all the ingredients except the syrup until thoroughly blended. If the mixture is a little too liquid, add an extra spoonful of flour.

2   Line an individual pudding basin with microwave film and pour in the mixture. Cover with kitchen paper and microwave on Medium for 1½ minutes.

3   Place the syrup in a bowl and microwave on high for 10-15 seconds.

4   Turn out the pudding on to a serving plate and pour over the syrup.

Fruity Baked Apple

Serves 1

Ingredients	Metric	Imperial	American
Apple	1	1	1
Sultanas (golden raisins) or raisins	15 ml	1 tbsp	1 tbsp
Soft brown sugar	15 ml	1 tbsp	1 tbsp
Butter or margarine	30 ml	2 tbsp	2 tbsp
Flaked almonds			

1   Core the apple and peel off a line of skin around the 'equator' of the apple. Stand it in a small dish.

2   Mix together the sultanas or raisins and the sugar and press into the centres of the apples. Dot with half the butter. Microwave on High for 1½-2 minutes.

3   Remove the apple from the microwave and leave to stand for 3 minutes.

4   Meanwhile, place the remaining butter and the flaked almonds in a bowl and microwave on High for 1-1½ minutes. Sprinkle over the apple to serve.

Rhubarb Crumble

Serves 1

Ingredients	Metric	Imperial	American
Rhubarb	*225 g*	*8 oz*	*½ lb*
Sugar	*15 ml*	*1 tbsp*	*1 tbsp*
Cornflour (cornstarch)	*5 ml*	*1 tsp*	*1 tsp*
Butter or margarine	*15 g*	*½ oz*	*1 tbsp*
Wholemeal flour	*15 g*	*½ oz*	*2 tbsp*
Porridge oats	*25 g*	*1 oz*	*¼ cup*
Demerara sugar	*25 g*	*1 oz*	*2 tbsp*

1 Place the rhubarb in a bowl and stir in the sugar and cornflour.

2 Rub the butter or margarine into the flour. Stir in the oats and sugar. Sprinkle over the rhubarb.

3 Microwave on High for 2-3 minutes.

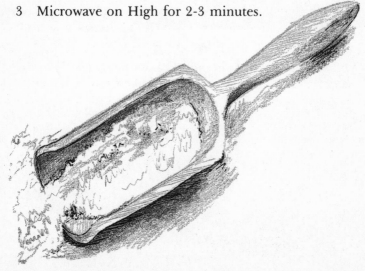

Caramel Oranges

Serves 1

Ingredients	Metric	Imperial	American
Caster (superfine) sugar	25 g	1 oz	2 tbsp
Cold water	15 ml	1 tbsp	1 tbsp
Warm water	15 ml	1 tbsp	1 tbsp
Brandy or orange liqueur	5 ml	1 tsp	1 tsp
Large seedless orange	1	1	1

1   Put the sugar and cold water into a small bowl and microwave on High for 3-4 minutes until the sugar has dissolved and created a golden caramel, stirring occasionally.

2   Stir in the warm water and microwave on High for 45-60 seconds until dissolved.

3   Finely grate the orange rind. Cut off the pith and outer membrane from the orange then slice the flesh thickly. Arrange the slices in a serving dish.

4   Stir the orange rind and brandy or liqueur into the caramel and pour over the orange. Chill well before serving.

Chocolate Mousse

Serves 1-2

Ingredients	Metric	Imperial	American
Plain (semi-sweet) chocolate	100 g	4 oz	¼ lb
Strong black coffee	25 ml	1½ tbsp	1½ tbsp
Brandy or rum	5 ml	1 tsp	1 tsp
Eggs, separated	2	2	2
Double (heavy) cream, whipped	60 ml	4 tbsp	4 tbsp

1   Grate 25 g/1 oz of the chocolate and break the remainder into pieces.

2   Place the pieces of chocolate into a bowl with the coffee and brandy and microwave on High for about 1 minute until melted, stirring once or twice during cooking.

3   Leave to cool slightly then blend in the egg yolks. Leave to cool.

4   Whisk the egg whites until stiff then fold them into the chocolate mixture. Pour into a soufflé dish and chill for at least 3 hours.

5   Decorate with whipped cream and the reserved grated chocolate.

Fresh Fruit Fool

Serves 1

Ingredients	Metric	Imperial	American
Dessert apple, peeled, cored and sliced	1	1	1
Grated rind and juice of orange	1	1	1
Soft brown sugar	15 ml	1 tbsp	1 tbsp
Egg white	1	1	1
Double cream	15 ml	1 tbsp	1 tbsp

1   Place the apple, orange rind and juice in a bowl, cover and microwave on High for 3 minutes. Leave to cool.

2   Purée the fruit in a blender or food processor. Stir in enough sugar to sweeten the fool to taste.

3   Whisk the egg white until stiff then fold it into the purée.

4   Serve topped with the cream and a sprinkling of sugar.

Chocolate and Marshmallow Treat

Serves 1

Ingredients	Metric	Imperial	American
Butter or margarine	*30 ml*	*2 tbsp*	*2 tbsp*
Digestive biscuit			
(Graham cracker) crumbs	*50 g*	*2 oz*	*½ cup*
Caster (superfine) sugar	*15 ml*	*1 tbsp*	*1 tbsp*
Milk chocolate, chopped	*75 g*	*3 oz*	*3 oz*
Large marshmallows	*6*	*6*	*6*
Milk	*30 ml*	*2 tbsp*	*2 tbsp*
Double (heavy) cream,			
whipped	*120 ml*	*4 fl oz*	*½ cup*

1   Place the butter or margarine in a small shallow dish and microwave on High for about 30 seconds until the butter melts.

2   Stir in the biscuit crumbs and press around the base and sides of the dish.

3   Microwave on High for 30 seconds to 1 minute until set. Leave to cool.

4   Place the sugar, chocolate, marshmallows and milk in a large bowl and microwave on high for 1-1½ minutes until melted, stirring several times during cooking. Add a little more milk if the mixture is very thick. Leave to cool then chill.

5   Stir the whipped cream into the chocolate mixture and spoon into the base. Chill until set.

Chapter Thirteen

CAKES, AND BISCUITS

If you are cooking for one, a standard-sized cake may spoil before you can enjoy it. Here are some recipes for cakes and bars which you can make in small quantities and enjoy as a teatime treat, or cakes which you can bake and then freeze in small quantities. There are also some biscuits which will keep for a while in an airtight tin.

Nutty Chocolate Cake

Makes 1 × 20 cm (8 in) cake suitable for freezing

Ingredients	Metric	Imperial	American
Flaked almonds	50 g	2 oz	½ cup
Butter or margarine, softened	175 g	6 oz	¾ cup
Soft brown sugar	175 g	6 oz	¾ cup
Eggs, lightly beaten	3	3	3
Clear honey	75 ml	5 tbsp	5 tbsp
Soured cream	150 ml	¼ pt	⅔ cup
Self-raising flour	175 g	6 oz	1½ cups
Cocoa powder (unsweetened chocolate)	30 g	1½ oz	6 tbsp
Ground almonds	30 g	1½ oz	6 tbsp
Granulated sugar	45 ml	3 tbsp	3 tbsp
Water	45 ml	3 tbsp	3 tbsp

1   Arrange the almonds on a plate and microwave on High for 4-5 minutes until golden, checking several times during cooking. Leave to cool.

2   Cream the butter and sugar until pale. Gradually beat in the eggs then blend in the honey and cream.

3   Sift together the flour and cocoa then fold the mixture into the bowl. Fold in the ground almonds. Spoon the cake mixture into a greased and lined cake dish and microwave on High for 10 minutes until cooked.

4   While still hot, sprinkle the cake with the toasted almonds.

5   Place the granulated sugar and water in a small bowl and microwave on High for 3-4 minutes until caramelised. Spoon over the surface of the cake. Leave to cool.

Lemon Cake

Makes 1 x 18 cm (7 in) cake suitable for freezing

Ingredients	Metric	Imperial	American
Self-raising flour	225 g	8 oz	2 cups
Pinch of baking powder			
Butter or margarine	100 g	4 oz	½ cup
Soft brown sugar	100 g	4 oz	½ cup
Eggs	2	2	2
Grated lemon rind	10 ml	2 tsp	2 tsp
Milk	15 ml	1 tbsp	1 tbsp
Lemon juice	30 ml	2 tbsp	2 tbsp
For the filling and icing			
Lemon curd	60 ml	4 tbsp	4 tbsp
Icing (confectioners')			
sugar	175 g	6 oz	1 cup
Lemon juice	15 ml	1 tbsp	1 tbsp
Water	15 ml	1 tbsp	1 tbsp

1   Sift the flour and baking powder into a bowl. Rub in the butter or margarine until the mixture resembles breadcrumbs. Stir in the sugar.

2   Beat the eggs into the mixture then stir in the remaining ingredients. Spoon into a greased and lined 18 cm (7 in) deep cake dish, stand the dish on an upturned plate and microwave on High for 5 minutes.

3   Leave to stand for 5 minutes then turn out and leave to cool. Freeze the cake before decorating.

4   Cut the cake in half horizontally and sandwich together with lemon curd.

5   Sift the icing sugar and gradually blend in enough lemon juice and water to make the icing. Spread over the top of the cake and leave to set.

Fruit Loaf

Makes 1 x 450 g/1 lb loaf suitable for freezing

Ingredients	Metric	Imperial	American
Plain (all-purpose) flour	175 g	6 oz	1½ cups
Baking powder	10 ml	2 tsp	2 tsp
Pinch of salt			
Butter or margarine	25 g	1 oz	2 tbsp
Soft brown sugar	30 ml	2 tbsp	2 tbsp
Egg, beaten	1	1	1
Natural yoghurt	150 ml	¼ pt	⅔ cup
Pinch of bicarbonate of soda (baking soda)			
Sultanas (golden raisins)	50 g	2 oz	⅓ cup
Raisins	25 g	1 oz	3 tbsp

1   Sift the flour, baking powder and salt into a bowl. Rub in the butter or margarine until the mixture resembles breadcrumbs.

2   Stir in the sugar, egg, yoghurt and bicarbonate of soda and mix to a soft dough. Stir in the fruit.

3   Spoon the mixture into a greased and lined 450 g/1 lb loaf tin and smooth the top. Microwave on High for 4-5 minutes. Leave to stand for 5 minutes before turning out.

Butter Shortbread

Serves 4

Ingredients	Metric	Imperial	American
Caster (superfine) sugar for sprinkling			
Butter, cold	100 g	4 oz	½ cup
Caster (superfine) sugar	50 g	2 oz	¼ cup
Plain (all-purpose) flour	175 g	6 oz	1½ cups

1   Grease a shallow 23 x 13 cm/9 x 5 cm dish and sprinkle with caster sugar.

2   Mix together the butter and sugar then work in the flour to form a soft dough.

3   Press the dough into the prepared dish and refrigerate for 30 minutes. Prick all over with a fork and mark into fingers.

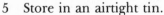

4   Microwave on High for 4-4½ minutes. Leave to stand for 10 minutes then turn out and cut into fingers. Sprinkle with caster sugar when cold.

5   Store in an airtight tin.

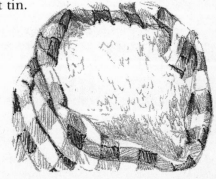

INDEX

Asparagus in Wine 55

Barbecue Sauce 75
Bean and Vegetable Salad 67
Beef and Mushroom Sauce 76
Beef Snack, Toasted 20
Beef Stew, Mediterranean 47
Beefburgers, Cheese-Stuffed 45
Broccoli and Cauliflower
    Salad 66
Brussels Sprouts with Lemon
    Butter 56
Butter Shortbread 94
Butterscotch Sauce 80

Caramel Oranges 86
Carrot Soup 9
Cheese Bread, Tasty 25
Cheese Sauce 74
Cheesey Smoked Mackerel 17
Chick Pea Pâté 15
Chicken with Goulash Sauce 39
Chicken Liver Pâté 16
Chicken Livers, Herbed 42
Chicken with Nutty Rice 40
Chicken with Spicy Sauce 38
Chicken Stir-Fry 41
Chilli con Carne 46
Chinese Meatballs 18
Chocolate and Marshmallow
    Treat 89
Chocolate Mousse 87
Cod with Olives 31
Cod with Tarragon, Orange 33
Corn on the Cob with Herb
    Butter 58
Courgette and Tomato Soup 10
Cucumber and Dill Sauce 76-7
Custard Sauce 80-1

Duck with Sharp Mustard
    Sauce 43

Eggs, cooking methods 21-2
Eggs with Salami, Baked 24
Emmenthal Fondue 28

Fried eggs 22
Fruit Fool, Fresh 88
Fruit Loaf 93
Fruity Baked Apple 84
Fruity Scallop Salad 64

Ham and Vegetable Potato
    Filling 62
Hard-boiled eggs 22
Hungarian Goulash 48

Kidneys in Wine 50

Lamb Chops with Mango
    Sauce 49
Lemon Cake 92-3
Lentil Soup with Bacon 11

Mackerel, Cheesey Smoked 17
Mackerel with Gooseberry
    Sauce 30
Minestrone Soup 12
Mushroom Sauce 74
Mushroom and Tomato Potato
    Filling 60
Mushrooms, Stuffed 19
Mustard and Honey
    Vegetables 59
Mustard Sauce, Sweet 79

Nutty Chocolate Cake 91

Onion Sauce 74

Onion Soup, Rich 13
Onion-Yoghurt Sauce 77
Orange Cod with Tarragon 33

Parsley Sauce 74
Pepper Noodles 70
Pepperoni Pasta 69
Piperade 23
Poached eggs 22
Pork, Sweet and Sour 53
Pork Chop, Spicy 52
Pork Chop with Raspberry
    Chutney 51
Potatoes Florentine 63
Prawn Curry 36
Prawn Potato Filling,
    Creamy 61
Prawn Sauce 75
Prawns, Spanish Rice with 72
Prawns, Spicy 35

Quiche Lorraine 26–7

Raspberry Sauce 81
Red Cabbage with Apple 57
Rhubarb Crumble 85
Rich Onion Soup 13
Rolled Sole 34

Scrambled eggs 22
Shallot Sauce 74
Spanish Rice with Prawns 72
Spiced Peach Butter 78–9
Spinach and Carrot Pasta 71
Sponge Pudding with Syrup
    Sauce 83
Stuffed Trout with Orange
    Sauce 32–3

Tomato Sauce 78
Tuna and Avocado Salad 65

White Sauce and
variations 73–4